Noah

Susan Martins Miller

Illustrated by
Ken Landgraf

BARBOUR
PUBLISHING, INC.
Uhrichsville, Ohio

ISBN 1-57748-654-4

Published by Barbour Publishing, Inc., P.O. Box 719, Uhrichsville, Ohio 44683 http://www.barbourbooks.com

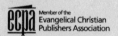

Member of the
Evangelical Christian
Publishers Association

Printed in the United States of America.

Noah

NOAH HAD A FUNNY FEELING.

1

The camel hair blanket scratched the old man's bearded cheek. After working in the fields all day, he should be tired. And his body was tired. His arms and legs ached from his labor. His neck was so stiff he could barely lift his head off the pillow. His eyes had been shut for a while, but behind his closed eyes, the old man's mind was wide awake. His brain churned out one thought after another.

Sighing, he pushed the scratchy blanket away from his face. Noah had a funny feeling. Something nagged at his brain. He was overlooking something important, but he could not figure out what it was. He knew he would never be able to sleep until he figured out what was keeping him awake.

In his mind, he went over the day. He had fed the livestock in the morning. The grain bin was almost empty, so he had looked for his son, Shem, to ask him to fill it. But he had not seen Shem all day. Noah would have to remember tomorrow to remind Shem, or the animals would have nothing to eat.

After tending the animals, Noah had gone out into the fields to inspect the crops. Ham and Japheth, his other two sons, met him there. They agreed that they would have a fine harvest this year. Nothing was wrong with the crops, and Shem would eventually remember to feed the animals. What was keeping Noah awake?

Sighing, Noah heaved himself over to one side. He was six hundred years old. He was an old man, a tired old man who still worked hard every day. He ought to be sleeping. Why wasn't he? He kicked at the blanket.

When he came in from the fields for the midday

HE HAD FED THE LIVESTOCK IN THE MORNING.

meal, his wife was flustered. She would not say why. Noah had stroked her back and tried to soothe her. He suspected she was worried about the missing Shem.

"Is his wife gone, too?" Noah asked.

His own wife grunted.

"It is nothing," Noah said softly. "They have gone off to spend the day together."

"There is work to be done," his wife answered. She poured thick soup into a dish. "I saw you feeding the animals this morning."

"And Shem will do his work," Noah said confidently.

"It is time for the boy to show some responsibility."

"He is not a boy. He is a man. All our boys are men," Noah reminded his wife. "They have their own wives. They have brought us the daughters we did not have. God has blessed us."

Noah's wife turned and looked him in the eyes. "I am always amazed at how deeply you believe in

SHE POURED THICK SOUP INTO A DISH.

God," she said. "When I look around, I see evil, pure evil. People are killing each other, cheating each other, lying, stealing, disobeying every law anyone ever made. Yet you believe God has blessed us."

Noah picked up a bowl of soup and set it on the table. "God has blessed us. All the things you say are true. Many days, I am as frightened as you are to leave the safety of our home." His eyes widened. "That is why you are concerned about Shem."

She turned away again and filled another bowl with soup. "What if he does not come back?"

"He will come back. He always does."

"What if today he does not?"

"God will keep him safe."

"Noah, you are closer to God than anyone I know. In fact, outside of our family, I do not know anyone who believes in God."

"God walks with me wherever I go." Noah broke off a piece of bread and said no more.

They ate their lunch in silence, listening for

"GOD WALKS WITH ME WHEREVER I GO."

any sound of Shem's safe return. He had not come home all day. Ham and Japheth and their wives did not know where the missing couple had gone.

Lying in the dark that night, Noah breathed in the sweet scent of his wife sleeping peacefully next to him. She had worried herself into exhaustion. It was the middle of the night, and she was sound asleep—just like she was supposed to be. Noah shook his head and turned over once more.

Then he heard it. His eyes, wide open, darted around the dark room. There it was again. He could not see it, but he knew something was there. Holding his breath, he listened. No one else would hear it. But Noah heard it.

He did not know how long it lasted. It might have been only a few seconds or several hours. Noah sat bolt upright, nearly knocking the blanket off the mattress he shared with his wife.

"Noah!" his wife said sharply.

"NOAH!" HIS WIFE SAID SHARPLY.

NOAH

Noah cringed. His wife did not like to be awakened in the middle of the night without a very good reason.

"What in the world is going on?" she demanded. "You are thrashing about like you are harvesting wheat. And all that sighing and moaning and singing—you're making too much noise."

"Singing? I was singing?" Noah asked.

"You always insist you have a song in your soul. But I don't understand why your soul cannot be quiet at night."

Noah smiled. If he was singing, then it was true. What he had heard was a holy moment.

"You are not going to believe what just happened," Noah told his sleepy wife.

"If I am not going to believe it anyway, you might as well wait for morning to tell me," she answered groggily.

"Yes, yes, in the morning," Noah agreed. "The boys, too. We must get the boys together."

"WHY DON'T WE INVITE THE NEIGHBORS TOO?"

"I thought you said they were men," his wife answered.

"Yes, and their wives. You must all know."

"Why don't we invite the neighbors, too? Perhaps they are interested in your middle-of-the-night adventures."

Noah paid no attention to his wife's harsh tone. "No, no, not the neighbors. No one from town. Just the family."

"Good. Just the family." His wife was drifting back to sleep. "Whatever you say. Just be still and let me sleep."

Noah patted his wife's shoulder. "Yes, I will try to be still."

He lay back down in the bed and crossed his arms across his chest. Now he was more awake than ever. What did it all mean? What God had said to him in the night was a message for a young man. *I am so old,* Noah told himself. *Perhaps I am losing my mind. Even if I were three hundred years younger, I would find this hard to believe.*

HE LAY BACK DOWN IN BED.

NOAH

But Noah had walked and talked with God every day for six hundred years. He knew when God spoke. And he knew that he would obey. No matter how ridiculous the message sounded, Noah would do what God asked him to do. He would need the help of his sons. The job was far too big for one old man. But he would obey.

Silently, he repeated to himself what he had heard. He said the words over and over. He no longer wanted to sleep. He wanted to remember every word.

HE WANTED TO REMEMBER EVERY WORD.

SHEM STOOD AMONG THE CHICKENS.

2

Noah plunged his hands into the water trough and splashed cool refreshment on his face. His sleepless night was catching up with him. But at least Shem had come home. When Noah went out to feed the animals in the morning, Shem was there. The feeding bins were full of grain. Shem stood among the chickens, throwing out handfuls of feed, singing as he worked.

Noah worked alongside Shem all morning. They tended the animals together and walked through the fields checking on the crops. Shem did not say where he had been, and Noah did not ask. He was just glad Shem had come home. Now he would be able to talk to all three of his sons and their wives at the same time.

The morning passed quickly. Now Noah was cleaning up for lunch. He could hear his wife scolding Shem for making her worry. Shem only laughed and kissed his mother sloppily on one cheek. Noah smiled at the familiar sight.

He had good sons, sons to be proud of. Nearly every time he went into town, Noah heard a new story about someone's son who had stolen or murdered someone else's son. He saw the bribes passed under the tables in the marketplace. He heard the lies that the merchants told so that they could sell more of their goods. He ached with other fathers whose sons ran off and never came home again. Yes, Noah had good sons. The Lord had blessed him.

Japheth stuck his head out the door and called, "Father, the meal is ready."

"I'll be right there," Noah responded. He

HE COULD HEAR HIS WIFE SCOLDING SHEM.

splashed his face one more time and then dried his hands and face on a clean cloth. As he turned to enter his home, he took a deep breath. Would his family believe what he had to say?

Inside, he took his seat. Around the table, his whole family was gathered. Shem, Ham, and Japheth sat with their wives. His own wife sat at the far end of the table. Before them was a meal of roasted lamb and bread.

Noah smiled at his family. "God has provided for us another day," he said. And they began to eat.

His wife raised the platter of meat and handed it to Ham. "Noah, are you going to explain what all that fuss was about in the middle of the night?"

Noah was caught off guard. He had expected to bring up the subject himself. His wife's question forced him to try to organize his thoughts.

Japheth put two thick slices of bread on his plate. "What fuss?" he asked. "I didn't hear anything."

"That's because you were not sleeping next to

NOAH SMILED AT HIS FAMILY.

your father," his mother answered.

Japheth turned toward Noah. "Is something wrong, Father?"

Everyone's eyes were fixed on Noah.

"No, no, nothing is wrong," Noah began. "But I do have something to tell you all. It's difficult to explain."

Shem passed the platter of lamb to his wife. "You might as well try, while we're all here."

Noah pushed his empty plate away. Suddenly he was not very hungry. He looked around the table, knowing that he should say something soon.

"What is it, Father?" Ham asked.

"God spoke to me last night," Noah said quietly.

"God? Are you sure?" Japheth asked.

"Yes, I'm sure. God has spoken to me before. I know the voice of the Almighty."

"What did he say?" Shem's wife asked.

Noah closed his eyes. "He said He is going to

"GOD SPOKE TO ME LAST NIGHT."

destroy the earth," he said quietly. "Every living creature will perish."

Around the table, no one spoke. Noah opened his eyes. His whole family was staring at him. He knew what they were thinking.

"I assure you, I have not lost my mind," Noah said firmly.

"Destroy the earth?" Ham said. "The entire earth?"

"That is what He said. Because the earth is filled with violence, God is going to destroy it. He gave me instructions to build an ark."

"An ark?" Japheth echoed.

"Yes, an ark. A big boat. A huge ship."

"Then not everything is to be destroyed," Shem said.

"We are to be spared," Noah said. "Only us. God is making a covenant with me. My wife, my sons, and my sons' wives will be spared. We will take with us into the ark two of every kind of animal, and seven of every kind of bird. After the

"HE GAVE ME INSTRUCTIONS TO BUILD AN ARK."

flood, the animals will breed and fill the earth again."

"Flood?" his wife asked.

"Yes, a flood," Noah answered. "God is going to bring flood waters on the earth to destroy every living creature, except what is in the ark."

"Just how big is this ark?" Ham asked.

"Very big," Noah answered. "It will be 450 feet long, seventy-five feet wide, and forty-five feet high. It will have a roof, of course, and we will build the sides of the ark up to within eighteen inches of the roof."

"That's big," Japheth agreed. "But the animals— we can't just throw them in that empty space."

"We'll build decks," Noah went on. "We'll have a lower deck, a middle deck, and an upper deck. Each deck will be divided into rooms. We'll have living quarters, of course. And the animals will be arranged in a way that keeps the smaller ones safe."

"With that many animals in one place, I hope

"GOD IS GOING TO BRING FLOOD WATERS."

we'll have windows for fresh air," Shem said.

"We'll have a row of windows just under the roof," Noah said, "and one door."

Noah looked around the table. His sons avoided his eyes. They looked at each other with questions in their eyes.

"I know what you are thinking," Noah said. "I am an old man, and I have had an old man's dream. You think that maybe the spicy stew last night upset my stomach and gave me nightmares. But this is no dream. Haven't I always told you the truth? I am telling the truth now."

"Of course you are, Father," Japheth said, after a long silence. "We know you would not tell us something you knew was a lie. It's just—"

"It's just incredible," Shem blurted out. "We need some time to understand what you are saying."

"I can repeat it, if you want me to," Noah said. "But we do not have much time. We must begin working right away."

"IT'S JUST INCREDIBLE," SHEM BLURTED OUT.

NOAH

"How long will we be in this ark?" Shem's wife asked.

Noah shook his head. "I don't know the answers to all your questions. We will take every kind of food that we can. We will need to begin storing food right away."

"What if it is not enough?" Shem asked. "We'll have all the animals to feed, too, after all."

"It will be enough. God always provides enough." Noah looked around the table. No one had eaten much of the carefully prepared meal. "I know this is incredible," he said. "You want to believe me, but it is hard. Don't believe me. Believe God. What He has said will happen."

"BELIEVE GOD!"

THEY BEGAN TO GATHER THE WOOD.

3

Noah dragged his arm across his forehead and wiped the sweat on his sleeve. He had never worked so hard in all of his six hundred years.

It had taken him days to calculate how much wood it would take to build the ark. Shem and Ham asked him where he planned to get that much wood. He told them it would be their responsibility to get it. He grinned as he said it. Their jaws dropped open in protest, and that made Noah laugh. But they began to gather the wood. First they bought as much as they could. They went to everyone they knew who might have a pile of wood and asked if they had any gopher wood for sale. If the wood was already cut, they could save a lot of work, although they still had to move it to their own property.

Next, they had to look for forests where they could cut the rest of the wood they needed. They hiked for days looking for just the right wood. Their father's instructions were very specific. It had to be gopher wood. They hired a team of strong young men with saws and axes. Ham and Shem marked the trees they wanted, and the men went to work. They chopped the trees, sawed them into flat boards, and hauled the wood to Noah's property.

Japheth helped his father at the work yard. Noah repeated the instructions for the ark so many times that Japheth knew them as well as his father. They had the same picture in their minds of what the ark would look like when it was finished. As the project grew, Japheth was amazed at how long 450 feet was. He himself felt smaller by the day.

THEY HIRED A TEAM OF STRONG YOUNG MEN.

They had fenced off a huge work yard. Now Japheth was sure the space would be too small.

Almost as soon as they began to build, Japheth convinced Noah that the job was too big for just the two of them. They hired day workers who came and followed their directions. At first, Japheth did not want to tell anyone what they were building. Who would believe them? On some days, he could hardly believe it himself. He trusted his father, but other people would not be so understanding.

Japheth just told the workers where to put the boards and how to fasten them together. He waited for the day when they would insist he answer their questions. The workers had many ideas about what the project might be. Japheth paid no attention to their guesses.

The day came when Noah and Japheth had to mix a huge vat of pitch. The tarry, smelly, sticky goo would make the ark waterproof. The workers put their tools down and lined up in

SOON THEY BEGAN TO BUILD.

front of Noah and Japheth.

"You must tell us what we are building," one of the men said. "You can't expect us to work with that awful stuff if you don't tell us what we are doing."

Japheth glanced at his father. "We're paying you to do what we tell you to do. You don't have to stay if you don't want to."

None of the men moved. The leader glared at Japheth.

"Hazar," Japheth said, "take your men and go back to work."

"Not until you tell us what we're building."

Japheth shook his head. He did not want to tell them. But Noah stepped forward.

"We're building an ark," he said, "and the pitch is to make it waterproof."

"An ark?" Hazar asked skeptically.

"An ark—a big, flat boat."

Some of the men began to snicker. "A boat this big?" one said. "We're nowhere near the ocean,

"WE'RE BUILDING AN ARK."

and you've never been a sailor. What do you need with a huge boat?"

"If you are really interested, I'll be happy to explain it to you," Noah said calmly. "But the news is not good."

"What news?"

"Father, please," Japheth said, laying his hand on his father's arm. "Please don't say anything more."

Noah turned to his son. He spoke quietly. "Don't you think we owe them an explanation?"

"We owe them nothing, except their wages," Japheth insisted.

"I know what you are thinking," Noah said. "Who will believe us? They will think we are a family of crazy people."

"What is the point of trying to explain?" Japheth said.

Noah shrugged. "We cannot do all this work ourselves. If we want them to stay, we must answer their questions."

"WE CANNOT DO ALL THIS WORK OURSELVES."

NOAH

"If we answer their questions, they will run in fear," Japheth said.

"Only if they believe us. I don't think they will." Noah spoke sadly.

"But they will laugh at us," Japheth said. "Listen. They have already begun to laugh at the mention of the ark."

"Let them laugh." Noah straightened his shoulders. He sighed and turned back to the workers. "We are building an ark because there is going to be a flood that will cover the whole earth. Everything that we know will be destroyed. Nothing will be left except what is in the ark. God has told me that—"

Noah could not finish what he started to say. The whole group had burst into laughter.

Hazar smirked at Japheth. "I can see why you did not want the old man to speak. A flood that destroys the whole earth?"

Behind Hazar, another voice roared. "Your father is a crazy old man, Japheth. But I thought

"YOUR FATHER IS A CRAZY OLD MAN."

better of you—until now."

"My father is—" Japheth started to speak, but his father touched his arm and shook his head.

"No, Japheth. You are right. They will not listen to the truth," Noah said sadly.

Hazar threw a log on the fire under the vat of pitch. The oozing mixture gurgled and popped. "If you are crazy enough to keep paying us to work on this monstrosity, then I guess we'll do it. But don't complain later that we tried to cheat you." The other men joined Hazar in a fresh round of laughter.

Japheth sighed. The men would no longer just follow his instructions. He would have to put up with their ridicule every day until the ark was done.

"Let's all just get back to work," Japheth said. He picked up a long stick to stir the pitch.

Snickering, the men returned to their tasks.

Japheth turned to his father. "We have a long time before this job will be finished. Shem and

JAPHETH STIRRED THE PITCH.

Ham haven't even found all the wood we need yet. How are we going to put up with everyone laughing at us? I'm sure they will be stealing from us every chance they get, too, and lying about everything they do."

Noah nodded. "I know, Japheth. I may be old, but I am not as foolish as they think I am. But I don't care if they laugh. I am obeying what God told me to do. That's all that matters."

"But what about the stealing and lying?" Japheth asked.

"Why does it matter? Have you forgotten what will happen when the flood comes?" Noah asked.

Japheth nodded. "The world will be destroyed."

"HAVE YOU FORGOTTEN WHAT WILL HAPPEN
WHEN THE FLOOD COMES?"

HE LEANED AGAINST THE THICK TRUNK.

4

Noah straightened his shoulders and tried to tell himself he was not tired. It was the heat that wearied him, he told himself. If he could just stand in the shade for a few minutes, he would feel better.

He raised one arm and wiped the sweat from his face with his garment. Squinting into the afternoon sun, he chose the tree he would stand under. Slowly, he shuffled toward the spreading cedar tree. Just thinking about its cool shade made him feel better. When he reached the tree, he sank down on the ground and leaned against the thick trunk. He would close his eyes just for a few moments. Surely that would refresh him.

Behind him, the workers continued their labor in the sun. The walls of the ark had risen, foot by foot, until they stood forty-five feet high. The last part of the walls was almost finished. Soon it would be time for the roof. Noah was pleased with the progress. He was sure he had followed every instruction God had given. Noah leaned his head back against the tree and closed his eyes.

Watching him, two of the workers laid down their tools.

"Look at him," one of them said. "It's only mid-morning, and he's worn out already."

"He's an old man," the other replied. "He has no business getting involved in a project like this."

"He's more than old," the first one answered. "He's old and crazy. All this talk about a flood is ridiculous."

"I wonder if we're not crazy, too. We keep coming back to work on his crazy boat."

"LOOK AT HIM."

"He doesn't like it when you call it a boat. It's an ark."

"Okay, but it's a crazy ark. Why do we keep working on it?"

"Because he keeps paying us. And he pays very well."

"He must be using up everything he ever saved in his whole life." The man laughed. "I wonder why his sons don't protest. It's their inheritance the old man is wasting."

The other man shrugged. "They don't seem to mind. They say none of them are going to need gold or silver after the flood."

"Won't they be surprised when they have nothing left and there is no flood. How could anything destroy the whole earth? Such a bunch of fools!"

Their voices faded as the two men picked up their tools and wandered back to their work.

Noah opened his eyes. He had heard everything they said. He did not blame them. If he were

"HOW COULD ANYTHING DESTROY THE EARTH?"

a strong young man who had not yet walked with God, he might think the same thing. Noah knew lots of other very old men who got some crazy ideas into their heads. They could not tell the difference between what was real and imaginary. Why should anyone think he would be any different? But he wasn't crazy. And the least he could do was work as hard as anyone else.

With a sigh, Noah pulled himself to his feet. He turned back to the work yard and tried to think what needed to be done. There was a stack of wood that should be moved closer to the fire under the bubbling, stinky pitch vat. He would work on that. No one else seemed to like to go near the pitch vat. Noah leaned down and began filling his arms with wood.

When he could barely see over the armload of wood, he added one more piece to the pile. Stumbling, he began to make his way toward the fire. Noah could feel the eyes of the younger men fixed on him as he passed them, slowly but steadily.

NOAH BEGAN FILLING HIS ARMS WITH WOOD.

He could see the fire, but it seemed like it was miles away instead of only a few yards. Maybe those younger men were right; maybe he was a silly old man. Why had he tried to carry so much at one time? Breathing heavily, he continued.

"Father, let me help you." Shem was beside his father and began snatching wood from Noah's arms. Noah did not protest. He let Shem take nearly the whole load, till he carried only four small pieces in his own arms. Together, they moved toward the fire and dumped the logs on the ground.

"Father, let's sit down and rest," Shem suggested.

Noah shook his head. "No, I just had a rest."

"But I need one," Shem insisted, "and I want to talk to you."

Noah reluctantly agreed. Side by side, they sat on a low bench.

Shem sighed.

"What is wrong, my son?" Noah asked.

"It's these men," Shem answered. "They think

"WHAT IS WRONG, MY SON?"

this is just another job. They believe that when the ark is finished, they will move on and find other work."

Noah shook his head. "It is sad."

"But you have said that everything will perish," Shem went on. "You said that God will destroy all life under the heavens, and every creature that has the breath of life in it."

"I only told you what God told me," Noah said. "It was not my decision to destroy the earth."

"But God chose to spare you," Shem continued, "and because He is sparing you, He is sparing me also. I can't help but think about what is going to happen to everyone else I know."

Noah let his shoulders sag and exhaled. "It is sad. But all these people have had their chance to know God. They have not chosen to walk with Him, as I have, and as you have."

"I know that is true, Father," Shem said. "I have no real friends, because I don't know anyone I can trust."

"YOU SAID THAT GOD WILL DESTROY ALL LIFE."

"Everyone is corrupt."

"You can't get anything done without a bribe. All the merchants try to cheat you. Every time a group of people gathers, a fight breaks out. Most of the time, somebody ends up dead."

"All of this displeases God. That is why He is going to destroy the earth."

"Shouldn't we be trying to convince people to change their ways?" Shem asked. "There is room in the ark for more, isn't there? Or we could make it bigger."

Noah shook his head sadly. "No. God has spoken. He has given the size of the ark, and He has said that only our family will enter the ark." He lifted his eyes. "Here comes your wife now."

Shem looked to see his wife lugging an animal skin, stretched and tanned. Besides the crew building the ark, another group of people worked at tanning animal hides.

"My wife tells me that we have almost enough hides for the roof now," Shem said.

"WE HAVE ALMOST ENOUGH HIDES FOR THE ROOF."

"Good," Noah responded. "We'll be ready for that soon. And the food supply?"

"The women are gathering grain. They have sacks and sacks of it, and baskets of fruits and vegetables. They have meat hanging to dry. We should have plenty to eat."

Noah nodded in satisfaction and raised his eyes to the sky. "It won't be long."

"THE WOMEN ARE GATHERING GRAIN."

"IT'S AN ARK."

5

The work yard was quiet. Still convinced that Noah had lost his mind, the men had taken their tools and gone on to another job. Their work for Noah was finished.

"We did exactly as he asked," said Hazar, the work crew leader, "and I've never seen an uglier boat in all my life."

"It's not a boat," someone corrected Hazar. "It's an ark."

"It's a monstrosity. No one can argue with that."

The men roared with laughter. Noah said nothing. He had grown used to the ridicule. What the work crew or the neighbors thought did not matter. What did matter was that the ark was done. The work crew had followed every detail, even though they thought it was ridiculous. They had done everything right.

Noah and his sons stood alone in the work yard. The enormous ark loomed over them.

Japheth kicked an empty bucket. "I suppose we should clean this mess up," he said. "They left wood shavings and scraps from the animal hides everywhere."

His brother Ham shrugged his shoulders. "Why should we clean up? We won't be here much longer."

Noah smiled and nodded, pleased that Ham understood. "Leave the mess, Japheth," Noah said. "Let's enjoy the sight of our finished work."

Noah and his three sons set their eyes on the ark itself. Compared to the massive gopher wood structure, they looked tiny and frail. If they all stood on each other's shoulders, so that they were

THEY LOOKED TINY AND FRAIL.

four-men tall, they would still reach barely halfway up the height of the ark. Shem had already remarked that running from one end of the ark to the other made him lose his breath.

The roof was covered in animal hides stretched across an enormous wooden frame. Tucked in just under the roof, a row of small windows would let in some fresh air. But they would not be able to see very much once they were inside the ark. The windows were too high up to look out without climbing up to them from the upper deck.

"It's not ugly," Noah said, smiling. "It's beautiful. Let's have a final look inside."

"Good," Shem said enthusiastically. "I was hoping you would say that." He turned to lead the way to the one and only door into the ark. The heavy, wide, wooden slab of a door swung down from its frame. When it was down, it formed a ramp. The four men walked up the ramp and entered the lower deck.

"We'll put the big animals down here." Noah

THE FOUR MEN WALKED UP THE RAMP.

reminded his sons of what they already knew. "Make sure that you distribute them evenly when we bring them in. We can't have them all at one end. We don't want to tip over in the first wind we face."

Noah's sons looked around the lower deck. They, too, were pleased with what they saw. Above them were two more decks. Each of the three decks was divided into dozens of rooms. Noah and Shem had planned how all the animals would be arranged. The more dangerous animals would be separated from the peaceful ones. The wolves would be nowhere near the lambs. And the birds would need a safe place to fly, a spacious room with a high ceiling. Some of the rooms were very small. Others had dividing walls and shelves to help organize the smaller animals.

Some of the rooms would be used for storing food, both for the family and for the animals. Japheth had suggested having storage rooms at both ends of each deck so that they would not

NOAH'S SONS LOOKED AROUND THE LOWER DECK.

have to carry the heavy sacks of animal feed on their shoulders very far. The family would have a few small rooms for living space. It would not be as nice as the homes they had now, but they would make the rooms as comfortable as possible.

The four men walked the length of the lower deck, inspecting every room. Noah took note of the places that still needed to be cleaned or where the workmen had not done a satisfactory job. Everything must be perfect before they brought the animals in.

"Let's go upstairs," Noah said, leading the way to the middle deck.

The rooms looked large and wide while they were empty. Ham shook his head. "I can hardly believe we can ever fill up all this space, even with two of every animal in the world."

"Don't forget," Shem added, "we have to have seven of every kind of bird."

Shem was in charge of collecting animals. His father turned to him for a report. "Are you finding

THE FOUR MEN INSPECTED EVERY ROOM.

all the animals we need, Shem?"

Shem nodded. "We've been working on getting the harder animals first. We can always find the common animals at the last minute, like rabbits and dogs and camels. We're right on schedule."

Japheth laughed. "We don't even know what the schedule is, do we, Father?"

Noah pressed his lips together thoughtfully. "No, I don't know the exact schedule. But it will not be long."

"Then we should begin loading supplies," Japheth said.

Noah nodded. "First thing in the morning. We'll start loading the food and supplies first. Do we have enough food gathered?"

It was Ham's turn to report. "It's hard to say if we have enough, since we don't know how long we'll be aboard."

"Father has already told us that the flood will last forty days and forty nights," Japheth said.

Ham nodded. "And then?"

"WE'VE BEEN WORKING ON GETTING
THE HARDER ANIMALS FIRST."

"And then what?"

"And then how long will it be before we actually see dry land? And will there be anything left for us to eat when this is all over?"

"Ham is right," Shem agreed. "We have no idea what we will find when the flood is over."

"Or where we will be," Noah said. "Remember, we'll be afloat all that time."

"And when we do find dry land," Shem continued, "we'll have to start all over again. No laughing neighbors to help build anything. No cheating merchants to sell us their goods. It will be just the eight of us starting all over again."

For a long time, no one said anything. During the construction, they had focused on building the ark. While they gathered food and supplies, they had thought of what they needed while they were in the ark. How could they imagine what life would be like after the flood was over?

Noah sighed deeply. "We must obey the Lord. You have many questions, and I cannot answer

"WE MUST OBEY THE LORD."

them. I only know we must obey the Lord."

Walking more slowly, the foursome climbed the stairs to the upper deck. Even on the top deck, the walls rose far above their heads.

"Perhaps we should have made the windows bigger," Japheth suggested, "so we could see out."

"And we'll need plenty of fresh air once the ark is full of animals," Ham added.

Noah shook his head. "No. These are the instructions that God gave. Who are we to think we could design a better ark?"

His sons had no response.

"Okay, then," Japheth finally said, "in the morning we will begin loading hay and feed for the animals."

Noah nodded. "We must be ready."

"PERHAPS WE SHOULD HAVE
MADE THE WINDOWS BIGGER."

NOAH WAS STANDING AMONG THE CHICKENS.

6

"Noah! We need a chicken for supper!" Noah's wife called from the fire where she stirred a pot.

Noah was standing among the chickens, feeding them.

"Well, my friends," he said, "I have to choose one of you. If I don't, she will."

Nine hens and three roosters clawed in the dirt. Furry yellow chicks chased after the bigger birds with tiny quick steps. They all pecked furiously at the bits of grain that Noah tossed at them.

"You might as well have a good supper before you become supper," Noah murmured. He tossed out some more grain. The fattest hen of the bunch scurried over and filled her mouth greedily. Noah chuckled. "My wife would be very pleased if I brought you home."

Noah reached into his worn leather pouch for one more handful of grain. As he stretched out his arm to scatter it, he stopped. His fist tightened around the grain, and he stood perfectly still.

"This is a holy moment," he whispered to himself.

He was not sure how long he stood there before he moved again. Minutes? Hours? Finally he realized he was holding his breath and let it out.

"Seven days!" he exclaimed loudly.

"Father?" said a voice behind him. Noah spun around to see Shem watching him.

"Are you all right, Father?" Shem asked.

"Seven days," Noah repeated.

"Seven days?" Shem echoed.

"That's right. Seven days."

"Seven days for what, Father?"

NOAH REACHED INTO HIS LEATHER POUCH.

Noah's eyes widened as he looked at Shem. "Until the flood begins, of course."

"The flood? Are you sure?" Excitement made Shem's voice rise.

Noah nodded vigorously. "I'm sure. The Lord just told me. We have seven days. We must be in the ark when the heavens open and the water begins."

"We can be ready," Shem assured his father.

"We have to be!"

"We just have to get organized," Shem continued. "The hay is ready. Ham started lining the stalls with it today."

"What about food for us?"

"Mother has a lot of meat hanging to dry. It should be ready. All the women have been grinding wheat, so we will have plenty of flour."

"Good. And what about the pairs?" Noah asked. "Do we have a male and female of every animal? That's the most important thing."

Shem shrugged. "A few of the animals are

"WE HAVE SEVEN DAYS."

tricky. I have a few more to find."

"We have only seven days, Shem."

"It will be enough. If only I could find a female red fox, one of the small ones."

"But I saw a fox nearby today," Noah said. "I was afraid it was going to get the chickens, so I shooed it off."

"As long as the chickens are out, the fox will not be far off." Shem began to scan the yard.

"She went into the woods," Noah said, pointing.

"Then I'm going into the woods," Shem said with determination. He turned away from the chickens and toward the woods.

Suddenly, Noah grabbed his son's arm. "There she is," he whispered. "The fox—I see her eyes right over there." Two brown fox eyes peered out from the edge of the woods. They were fixed on the fat hen that Noah had chosen for supper.

Shem looked where his father pointed. "I see," he whispered. "Here I go."

Shem moved stealthily toward the edge of the

"THERE SHE IS."

wood. On his way, he picked up a length of rope. Smoothly but quickly, he moved across the yard, keeping his eyes fixed on the fox's eyes. He had been catching animals since he was a small boy. That was why Noah had given Shem the job of rounding up the animals. With one swift motion, he could snatch up the small animal and put a rope around its snout.

Noah held his breath as he watched his son. Shem had almost reached the fox. With the rope in one hand, Shem dove at the fox. Her tail brushed in his face as she scampered out of reach. Shem landed face down in the dirt. He groaned loudly.

Noah did not know whether to laugh or sigh. They needed that female fox, and he wanted Shem to catch her. But the sight of his determined son with his face in the dirt made him chuckle. Shem stood up, brushed himself off, and headed into the woods.

Noah turned back and crossed the yard toward his home. "Ham, Japheth," he called as he walked.

SHEM DOVE AT THE FOX.

"Get your wives. I need to talk to everyone."

No one answered. "Ham! Japheth! Get your wives!" Noah called again.

Finally the small group gathered, curious about what Noah had to say this time.

"The flood will begin in seven days," Noah announced. "We have seven days to prepare."

His wife scoffed. "Seven days! We have far too much to do. We cannot be ready in seven days. The vegetables will not be ready."

Noah laughed. "Do you think God is going to hold back the heavens because your vegetables are not ready?"

"Why didn't you tell me sooner?" his wife countered.

"I didn't know until just now," Noah answered. "We have one week. We must be ready." He turned and looked across the big yard. "I'm going to walk through the ark one last time. I want to be sure we are not forgetting anything."

"I'll tell you what you've forgotten," his wife

NOAH LAUGHED.

said. "You've forgotten our supper."

"Oh, yes, the chicken," Noah answered. "I have a hen picked out."

"We need that chicken in the pot soon."

"You'll have it," Noah assured his wife. He himself did not have much appetite. There was far too much to think about. He hardly wanted to take time to eat.

"I'll go with you, Father," Japheth offered. "We need to take a look at the upper deck. I think we need some more shelves in the stalls in the stern."

"Come along, then." Noah and Japheth started across the yard toward the ark.

"Where is Shem?" Japheth asked.

"Catching a fox," Noah answered.

Japheth chuckled. "The small female fox? He's been after one for weeks."

"Today is the day he'll catch her," Noah said, grinning. "He knows he's running out of time." He raised his eyes toward the woods. "There he is now."

"THERE HE IS NOW."

Shem had indeed caught the fox. Her snout was muzzled with his rope, but she squirmed in his muscular arms. The look of determination on Shem's face told Noah that his son would not let the fox get away. However, Shem was covered in dirt, and his clothing was torn.

Japheth threw his head back and roared at the sight of his brother. "If you show up for supper looking like that, Mother will throw you in the pot instead of the chicken!"

Shem grinned in triumph. The small red fox thrashed in his arms.

"The pen is ready," Japheth said. "You'd better put her in with the others before she gets loose and grabs the chicken she's been after."

"The chicken!" Noah exclaimed. He whirled and scurried across the yard. "I must get the chicken!"

THE FOX SQUIRMED IN SHEM'S ARMS.

"ARE YOU SURE THE AARDVARK IS FEMALE?"

7

"Are you sure that aardvark is female?" Japheth looked suspiciously at the scaley animal his brother had just penned up. "It looks just like the other one to me."

Shem sighed. He latched the gate to the pen. "I'm as sure as I can be," he answered.

"But what if you're wrong?" Japheth challenged. "If we don't have a pair to mate and breed, there won't be any more aardvarks when this is all over."

"Perhaps you would like to have a closer look," Shem suggested, "so you can see for yourself."

"Oh, I trust you," Japheth said quickly. "You're far more familiar with the animal species than I am."

Shem nodded. If Japheth trusted him, why was he asking questions about the aardvarks?

Everyone was tired. The seven days had passed too quickly. No one slept very much. Instead, they exhausted themselves day and night. Strings of dried meats and vegetables, mounds of hay and grain, cooking pots, firewood, clothing, bedding, tents, furniture—they had to take everything they could. Nothing would be left when they found dry land again.

And the animals! Shem had been rounding them up for weeks, but they kept coming. There were too many animals even for the large work yard. Shem had begun to move them inside. Hundreds were already in the ark.

From time to time, an animal they had never seen before turned up in the work yard outside the ark. They always showed up in pairs. When that

SHEM HAD BEGUN TO MOVE THEM INSIDE.

happened, Shem added them to the list.

Sometimes he did not know what to call the strange creatures that appeared suddenly, so he made something up. In the last few days, he had gotten used to turning around and finding a male and female of some animal standing outside the ark. It was as if they were waiting to be told what to do. Birds, mammals, reptiles—Shem kept a careful account of everything he had. And he was sure he had a female aardvark. But maybe he could be more sure.

"I'll look again, Japheth," Shem said. He leaned on the fence and surveyed the pen of animals. "It can't hurt to double check."

Japheth slapped his brother on the back. "Thanks, Shem. I know Father will appreciate the extra effort, too."

"Where is Father?" Shem asked.

"In the ark," Japheth answered. "Mother has some very particular ideas about how she wants the furniture arranged. Father and Ham are trying

SHEM KEPT A CAREFUL ACCOUNT OF THE ANIMALS.

to make her happy."

Shem smiled and nodded.

"I hope she's happy with the cooking area," Japheth said. "We put it on the upper deck so the smoke might have somewhere to go. But the windows are small and very high."

"It will be fine, I'm sure," Shem said. "Mother will get used to it. We're all grateful to have the ark, considering what is coming." He lifted his eyes to the horizon.

Japheth followed his brother's gaze. The sky was heavy and gray. They had not seen the sun for nearly a week. Each day grew colder and more gloomy than the day before.

"Father says water will come from the sky and the ground," Shem said.

Japheth nodded. "It will last for forty days and forty nights. That's a lot of water!"

"It's hard to imagine what it will be like," Shem said softly. "We have only a few more hours."

THE SKY WAS HEAVY AND GRAY.

"Then perhaps we'd better get started with the rest of these animals," Japheth suggested.

Shem nodded. "Let's start with that pen over there," he said, pointing.

"The big cats," Japheth said, scowling.

"Yes, the lions, the tigers, the panthers, the cheetahs, the leopards," Shem said. "But don't worry, Japheth. They have become very gentle the last few days. It's as if they understand that something incredible will happen. They will give us no trouble."

"What happened to the elephants and camels?" Japheth looked at an empty pen.

"I loaded them this morning," Shem answered. "They are in the lower level. We'll put the cats at the other end."

They began the parade of animals: the cats were followed by the small furry animals, and after them came the amphibians. Shem had made a special tank for them so that they could have the water they need, but also have a bit of indoor land. The

SHEM HAD MADE A SPECIAL TANK.

birds came next—toucans and parakeets and parrots and blue jays and cardinals and robins and crows and swallows and doves and pelicans and wrens and pigeons and quail and ducks and swans. Then the ravens, eagles, falcons, black kites, horned owls, screech owls, great owls, gulls, hawks, ospreys, cormorants, storks, heron, and hoopoe and dozens of others.

"How do you keep them all straight?" Japheth asked as he ducked to avoid a swooping seagull.

Shem shrugged. "They all look different."

"I suppose you say the same thing about your bug collection."

Shem grinned. "Something like that." He had carefully sealed off space on the top deck for the insects. Fortunately, he could fit thousands of insects in a very small space: crickets and katydids, grasshoppers and bees, lady bugs and centipedes, spiders by the dozens, butterflies by the hundreds. Some of the bugs he had never seen before; they just appeared in the room. He stopped

THE BIRDS CAME NEXT.

trying to count them.

After checking on the monkeys and apes and the oxen and goats on the middle deck, Shem and Japheth went back outside. They planned to bring in the cattle and sheep next. They did not expect to see what they saw.

Japheth's eyes grew wide. "They've all lined up, Shem!" He looked at the lines of animals. The animal pens were open, and the animals were lined up in pairs: gerbils and guinea pigs, hamsters and rabbits, zebras, hippos, and rhinoceroses, black bears, brown bears, raccoons, skunks, squirrels, llamas, big horn sheep. The line seemed like it would never end.

"Shem, where did you find all these animals?" Japheth asked.

Shem was so surprised himself that he could hardly breathe. "I didn't," he said. "I found a few of them, but some of them I've never seen before. I don't even know what to call them."

Stunned, the two brothers watched as the

"THEY ALL LINED UP."

animals paraded toward the ark: kangaroos, pandas, penguins, ostriches, tortoises, bison, deer, gazelles, ibex, antelope.

Japheth laughed. "Even if we don't know what to call them, they're coming with us."

"Two of every kind of animal," Shem said. "That's what God told Father. I guess He didn't mean just the ones I knew."

Noah appeared in the doorway of the ark. A panda was curious about him and swatted at him. Noah ducked away from the great paw.

"Shem, what is that?" Noah called out. He moved to the side of the ramp so that the parade of animals could continue. "How do they all know what to do?"

Shem shrugged. "It's out of my hands now, Father. I think we're just supposed to wait."

"They'd better stay out of Mother's kitchen," Japheth said, "or she'll fix one of them for supper."

Noah laughed. "Somehow I think they'll end up just where they should be. The two of you

A PANDA SWATTED AT NOAH.

should come aboard, too."

Shem and Japheth followed their father back up the ramp and into the ark.

Noah glanced at the darkening sky. "It won't be long now."

NOAH GLARED AT THE DARKENING SKY.

"WE'RE ALL HERE."

8

"Are we all here?" Noah asked, looking around the small kitchen his wife had organized. Large cooking pots hung on hooks above his head. He reminded himself that he would have to duck every time he walked through the kitchen.

"Four men, four wives," his wife answered. "We're all here."

"Shem, have the animals finished loading?"

"I think so," Shem answered, nodding. "For awhile, new ones kept showing up every few minutes, but I think they've stopped coming. There haven't been any new ones for several hours."

"Then it's time to close the door," Noah answered somberly. "Ham, you come with me, and we'll close the door."

Together, father and son made their way down to the lower deck to the only door the ark had. They were ready to pull on the long, thick ropes and heave the heavy door up and closed. Then they would cover it with pitch to seal out the water.

"Father, look!" Ham said as they approached the door. He stopped in his tracks and pointed.

Noah nodded slowly. "The door is already sealed. God has closed it Himself."

"Then there is nothing for us to do."

"That's right. God has done it all. Let's go back to the others."

On the upper deck once again, the eight members of the family sat in a close circle. The air was chilly even inside the ark.

"Now what?" someone asked.

"Now the rain," Noah answered.

They sat in silence for a long time.

"GOD HAS CLOSED IT HIMSELF."

NOAH

"Will it come soon?" one of the wives asked. Noah nodded.

Silence came once again. Then the dripping sound started. *Pitter, pitter, patter. Pitter, patter.*

Ham raised his eyes to the high row of small windows above them. "I wish we could see out."

Noah shook his head. "There is no need to see out. What God is doing for us, He will do inside here."

"It's growing dark," Noah's wife said. "Perhaps we should light a lamp."

Noah nodded. The rain was falling steadily. The ground was parched with thirst and would soak up the waters eagerly at first. The ark was huge and heavy with the weight of the animals. Noah knew it might be days before they would feel the ark lift and begin to float. More days would pass before the neighbors who had made fun of him would know that Noah had been right after all. The rains were not going to stop, not for forty days and forty nights.

THE RAIN WAS FALLING STEADILY.

NOAH

Outside, the sky cracked open with a bolt of lightning. Inside, everyone jumped at the sound. Thunder roared and rattled the vessel. Water poured from the heavens and struck the ark with a force that rocked it. Noah caught hold of a table to balance himself.

"Everyone sit down and hold on to each other," Noah called out above the thunder.

With a great groan, the earth beneath them split, and water gushed out of the great crack and swirled ferociously around the ark.

"What was that?" Shem's wife asked anxiously.

"The springs of the great deep have burst forth," Noah told her. "Everything is happening just the way God said it would."

The ground under them creaked open wider. The family huddled around one small lamp for the longest time. The storm raged around them. The air coming in the high row of windows was damp and cold, but the overhanging roof kept out the water. Inside, the family was dry and safe.

THE STORM RAGED AROUND THEM.

"The animals will need to be fed," Noah said a few hours later.

Shem swallowed hard. "I guess we'll find out now whether our system is going to work. Ham, Japheth, come with me. I'll show you what to do."

Two days passed. Tending to the animals kept all eight members of the family busy. Feeding them, bringing fresh rain water to drink, and cleaning out the stalls was tedious work. But there was little else to do for the next forty days, so they worked side by side and kept up with the chores. Noah's wife kept a small fire burning in the kitchen for warmth and cooking.

On the third day, Shem and Noah were feeding the small animals on the upper deck.

"What was that?" Shem asked suddenly. He tilted his head to listen for the sound once more. The raging storm made it hard to hear anything. He put down his bag of nuts and moved to the wall of the ark. Turning his ear to the wall, he

SHEM AND NOAH FED THE SMALL ANIMALS.

listened again. "There it is again!"

"Noah!" came a faint voice. "You were right. Let us in!"

"Did you hear that?" Shem asked his father.

Noah hung his head. "The neighbors," he said softly.

"What should we do?" Shem asked. "Shall we make room for a few more?"

Noah shook his head sadly. "No, we cannot do that. God said only the eight of us would survive."

Shem opened his mouth to say something, then closed it. What could he say? His father was right. As the rumor spread about the ark project, hundreds of people had heard about it. And they had all laughed, every single one of them. No one believed what Noah said. No one believed in God. Besides, the door to the ark had been sealed, and the windows were too small and too high for anyone to crawl through.

The cries from outside came again, pleading to be allowed to enter.

THE PEOPLE PLEADED TO BE ALLOWED TO ENTER.

"How long will they stay out there?" Shem wondered aloud.

Noah shrugged. "They will soon leave us and look for higher ground."

"I feel sorry for them, Father. Am I wrong to feel sorry for people whom God wants to punish?"

Noah shook his head. "You have a tender heart, Shem, a compassionate heart. It's not easy to listen to their cries. But we built this ark and loaded all the animals because we believed God and wanted to obey Him. We cannot change our minds now."

"You're right, of course," Shem answered his father. Sadly, he picked up his bag of animal food. Just then lightning split the sky once more and the storm grew even louder. Shem could no longer hear the cries of his neighbors. He tossed a handful of nuts at the squirrels.

"Do these animals never sleep?" Noah asked as he stared at a raccoon. "They're always hungry."

The male squirrel scampered up the wall of

"DO THESE ANIMALS EVER SLEEP?"

the room and perched on a high shelf. Soon the female joined him. Holding a nut in her tiny hands, she gnawed on it.

"I never knew how much rabbits could eat," Shem said. "We only brought two rabbits aboard, but I have a feeling we'll have quite a few more before this journey is over."

Noah laughed. "We'll have more of a lot of things. But that's what God wants. The animals are supposed to multiply when we find dry land again. Some of them are just getting a head start."

The sky cracked open once more. Neither Shem nor Noah flinched this time. After listening to the ear-splitting thunder for three days, they were all used to it. The rumbling of the skies never seemed to fade away completely. Wherever they were inside the ark, they could hear the storm raging outside. The water poured down in steady, heavy sheets of rain. Everything was damp all the time. But there was no point in complaining, so no one did. After all, this was only the beginning.

THE STORM RAGED OUTSIDE.

THE ARK BEGAN TO SWAY GENTLY.

9

The days passed slowly. But every once in a while, something exciting happened. Noah and his wife were standing in the little kitchen when they felt the ark lift and pitch slightly to one side. Others felt it, too. Their sons came running down the wide, wooden hallway of the upper deck, and their wives dashed in from their work cleaning stalls. They all stood together as they felt the vessel lift off the ground and begin to float. The ark began to sway gently in the rising water.

"Now our journey truly begins," Noah said.

"And we find out if those workmen were

worth what we paid them," Japheth remarked.

They inspected the ark from stern to bow and side to side. They found no leaks. The vessel was sturdy and well-constructed.

Gradually, they got used to the motion of rocking in the water. They learned how to walk without losing their balance. Japheth and Ham tied down any supplies that might slide across the decks.

First one week went by, then the second one and the third. Noah and his family fell into a routine of tending the animals. Shem's system for feeding and cleaning seemed to be working. No area of the ark was neglected. The right kinds of food for the animals on each deck were stored in places that were easy to get to. Each day's schedule called for certain animal stalls to be cleaned. The job was a big one. Thousands of animals kept them busy every minute of the day.

When they were not working, the family

NOAH AND HIS FAMILY FED THE ANIMALS.

enjoyed eating their meals together. They had only each other for conversation. They told each other everything they did and everything they observed.

"The monkeys are starting to smell," Ham said one day, scrunching up his nose. "We'll have to clean their stalls more often."

Shem nodded. "I agree. I will change the schedule."

"We should throw some rain water at them," Japheth's wife suggested. "They need a bath."

"We can get all the rain water we need," Ham said confidently. He had rigged up a system to set out a basket on the upper deck and pull it in through one of the windows when it was full of water. A tall ladder allowed Ham and his brothers to climb up to the corner window and peek out under the edge of the roof. They could not see very much, but at least they could get water whenever they needed it.

"I didn't know the birds would be so noisy!"

"WE CAN GET ALL THE RAIN WATER WE WANT."

Shem said. "When they are outside, their little noises are soothing and pleasant. But when they are cooped up inside and all together in one place, the racket is not so nice."

"And the woodpecker!" Japheth added. "He's going to peck right through the wall one of these days. It echoes up and down the decks. He makes so much noise, and he pecks all day long. I wish he would be more quiet."

"He is simply doing what God created him to do," Noah said, chuckling. "A woodpecker must peck wood."

"Does he have to do it all the time?" Japheth asked.

Noah laughed. "It is a nuisance. But the day will come when we leave the ark, and you'll be sorry to see him go."

Japheth looked doubtful. He did not care if he ever saw another woodpecker.

"I've lost count of the days," Shem said. "Is this day twenty-five or twenty-six?"

"HE IS SIMPLY DOING WHAT
GOD CREATED HIM TO DO."

"Actually, this is day twenty-seven," Japheth informed him. "I've been marking the days off by scratching on the wall on the middle deck."

Ham laughed. "It looks like the woodpecker is not the only thing pecking wood."

Even Japheth smiled at that. "At least my scratchings have a purpose. And I don't keep anyone awake at night by doing it."

"Day twenty-seven," Shem repeated thoughtfully, "and it is going to rain for forty days. We're more than halfway through."

Japheth shook his head. "This is only the beginning. It will be weeks, maybe even months, before we find dry land."

"Do you really think it will take that long for the water to run off?" Shem asked.

His brother nodded. "There is nowhere for the water to go. By now the earth must be soaked very deeply. It will take a long time to dry out."

"We must be sure the land is safe for the animals," Noah reminded his sons. "They share the

"THIS IS ONLY THE BEGINNING."

job of rebuilding the earth."

"We have a long wait ahead of us," Japheth insisted.

"Well, we have plenty of supplies," Ham said, "and the smaller animals are already breeding, so we'll have chickens and rabbits to eat."

Shem turned to his father. "Where do you think we will end up, Father?"

Noah smiled slightly. "We will end up exactly where God wants us to be."

"But where will that be?" Shem pressed. "Will we be anywhere near our home?"

Japheth jumped in. "I don't think so, Shem. The waters are rising fast and moving fast. We are not staying in one place. We are floating farther from home every day."

"It won't matter," Ham said. "There will be nothing left at home anyway. We're all that's left by now."

No one spoke for a long time after that. It was hard to imagine leaving the ark and finding

"WE'LL HAVE CHICKENS AND RABBITS TO EAT."

no one else alive.

The rain came steadily. On some days, the sky broke open with a storm, and the wind swept the ark in circles. Lightning cracked the night, and thunder rumbled from one end of the ark to the other. On other days, the rain was calmer. But it was always heavy. And it never stopped. Whether they were sleeping, eating, feeding the animals, or talking to each other, the eight people in the ark always heard the sound of the rain in the background. During a storm, they simply raised their voices so others could hear them.

Noah found time to be by himself. Each evening after the chores were done for the day and the rest of the family had found their beds, he walked to the other end of the upper deck. The eyes of the animals watched him in the dark, until he came to his favorite spot. There he would listen to the rain. And some nights he would hear the voice of God in the storm. He would stay and listen for God to speak in the rain until he was again

THE SKY BROKE OPEN WITH A STORM.

full of assurance that God was taking care of him and his family. Then Noah would return to his mat on the floor next to his wife and sleep peacefully, no matter how much thunder rumbled outside.

NOAH WOULD SLEEP ON HIS MAT.

THIRTY-SEVEN DAYS HAD PASSED.

10

Japheth let his fingers slide gently over his markings in the hall of the middle deck. He counted softly under his breath, just to make sure. He counted thirty-seven marks. For thirty-seven days the rain had deluged the earth. For thirty-seven days the animals had cheeped and growled and chirped. For thirty-seven days they tooted and thumped and quacked. They baaed, hissed, and gobbled. They woofed, meowed, mooed, and cuckooed. And the woodpecker pecked wood. For thirty-seven days, the woodpecker pecked. For thirty-seven days, Japheth wished the woodpecker would stop pecking wood.

Noah came out of the stall where the goats and big horn sheep were. He was careful to close the gate securely behind him. The last thing he needed was for any of the animals to get loose and stir up chaos on the decks of the ark.

Noah walked slowly over to where Japheth stood. "Day thirty-seven," he said.

Japheth rubbed the wall. "That's right, day thirty-seven."

"Three more days, then," Noah said, "and the change will come."

Japheth grinned at his father. "I'd like to know if the change will make the woodpecker stop pecking wood."

Noah laughed. "I told Ham to put an extra post in the aviary."

"Father, you're just encouraging the woodpecker to keep going."

"It's better if he pecks at a post than if he

NOAH CLOSED THE GATE.

knocks a hole in the wall."

"I suppose you're right."

The animals did not know the difference as day thirty-seven became day thirty-eight and then day thirty-nine. But the family's excitement grew. Noah's wife suddenly had the urge to straighten up the living quarters and scrub them till they were spotless. Shem strolled the decks with his wife, humming cheerful melodies. Ham made a fresh list of the supplies they had left.

When Japheth woke on day forty, he heard the same steady background sound that he had heard for the thirty-nine days before. Wind swirled around the ark, and the water came down in sheets. At first, he wanted to find his father and ask a hundred questions. But he didn't. He just reminded himself that God had said it would rain for forty days and forty nights. One more day. That night would be the fortieth night. Surely in the morning, the rain would stop, Japheth told himself.

NOAH'S WIFE SCRUBBED THE FLOOR.

When Japheth woke on day forty-one, he again heard the gray, dull sound of the rain. He went to find his father. Noah was standing on the top deck, with his eyes raised to the high windows.

"This is the day, isn't it, Father?" Japheth asked.

Noah nodded.

Shem appeared on the deck. Soon Ham joined them, too. And then the women came. All eight of them stood in a small clear area on the top deck. They were in the corner where Ham had rigged a ladder. No one spoke very much. What was there to say? They were waiting for the rain to stop. It was the only thing that mattered right then. They watched the small windows for any sign of change in the weather.

After a long time, Noah's wife said, "I suppose I might as well go fix lunch. This day sounds like every other day."

Noah shook his head. "No. Today will be different."

"TODAY WILL BE DIFFERENT."

NOAH

"So far, it is the same, old man," his wife answered. She shuffled across the deck. "Waiting makes me hungry. I'm going to go make soup."

Her feet scraped along the wooden floor, making the planks squeak. But Noah was not listening to his wife's shuffling. He was hearing a different sound.

"There!" Noah cried. "The wind has stopped. It is not howling. The air is still for the first time in forty days."

Everyone stood perfectly still, including Noah's wife. They tilted their heads and listened.

"And the rain has stopped," Noah continued. "I hear only the water lapping up against the side of the ark. But I don't hear rain."

Shem pointed at a window. "Look, sunlight! The sun is coming out!"

Seven other heads turned to the high corner window. The roof of the ark, made out of leather hides, hung over the window and cast a thin shadow. But the air around the window was

"LOOK, SUNLIGHT!"

definitely filled with light.

"I want to see!" Ham blurted out, and he scrambled up the ladder he had built in the corner.

"Hurry," his mother said. "Tell us what you see."

Ham reached the top swiftly. He hoisted himself up and stretched his neck out as far as he could.

"All I see is water," he called back to the others.

"Forty days of rain and he expects to see land?" Japheth said, laughing.

"I see more water than I could ever imagine," Ham said. "It's an ocean out there. We're floating in the middle of an ocean!" He pulled himself back inside the ark and turned to his brothers. "I knew the flood waters would cover the earth," he said, "but I just never imagined what it would look like. It will be months before we see land again."

"But the sun is shining, right?" Shem asked.

Ham nodded. "Yes, the sun is shining—very brightly. There's not a cloud in the sky."

"ALL I SEE IS WATER."

NOAH

Noah nodded with satisfaction. "Of course the sun is shining. Of course there are no clouds. God said the flood would stop after forty days. Did any of you doubt that the sun would shine again?"

His sons shook their heads.

"Of course we knew the sun would shine," Japheth said, "but it still feels good to see it."

The others nodded. Even Noah had to agree that the sunlight was welcome.

"Now do you want some lunch?" Noah's wife asked the rest of the family.

"We'll help you," her daughters-in-law said.

"I'm so excited, I could eat a cow," Japheth said.

"Don't even think about it," Noah said, laughing. "We won't slaughter any animals until they have a chance to breed properly."

"I have some special cakes," Noah's wife said. "We'll have them with our soup for a celebration."

Noah's wife, his sons, and their wives moved toward the other end of the upper deck, where

"I HAVE SOME SPECIAL CAKES."

their living quarters were. Noah watched all seven of them walk away.

"Thank You, Lord, for sparing my family," he said softly. "We are safe in Your care. If it rained another forty days and forty nights, we would still be safe in Your care."

When his family was out of sight, Noah sighed with satisfaction. He knew that in only a few minutes his wife would call him to lunch. But for now, he only wanted to look up at the window one more time and see the beam of light that seemed to fall right on his face.

THE BEAM OF LIGHT FELL ON HIS FACE.

THE ELEPHANTS SCREECHED.

11

The woodpecker's beady little eyes glared at Japheth. Japheth's dark brown eyes stared back at the bird. In his mind he dared the little creature to go back to drilling his way through a log hung on a hook in his cage. The bird had been quiet for the last few days, and Japheth wanted things to stay that way. He tossed an extra handful of grain on the floor of the cage. Perhaps the woodpecker would want to eat and forget about pecking.

The din of the animals got on Japheth's nerves. The elephants screeched, the ducks honked, the lions roared, the beavers buzzed, the hippos sloshed around in their indoor mud. The tigers snarled, the pigs oinked and snorted, the camels brayed, the horses neighed, the cows mooed, the birds flapped and twittered. The crickets croaked, the bees buzzed, the monkeys chattered. And the woodpecker pecked wood.

During the weeks of rain, Japheth's head had been filled with the sounds of the raging storm. Now he heard animals every minute of the day, every day of the week. His head rang with noise, and there was nowhere to go to escape it. Sometimes he just wanted a bit of peace and quiet. How long would it take for the earth to dry up so that they could leave the ark?

The woodpecker ignored Japheth's offering of extra grain. The little eyes stayed fixed on Japheth.

"Have it your way," Japheth said aloud. "Eat, or don't eat. It doesn't matter to me." He turned to move on up the deck to the next set of animals waiting for their dinner.

Suddenly a roar of air drowned out all of the

THE CAMELS BRAYED.

animal noises. Japheth dropped his feed bag and put his hands over his ears. Never in his life had he heard such a sound. It was like a wind—but much greater than even the fiercest wind during the weeks of rain. *Will there be another storm?* Japheth wondered. Would the rains return and batter them once more? "Father!" Japheth called out. Leaving his grain bag behind, he began to walk up the main aisle, looking for his father.

The ark rocked violently from side to side. Japheth tumbled to the floor. He tried to scramble to his feet again, but instead, he slid backward. The front of the ark was raised much higher than the rear. The animals screamed in protest as they were thrown against the walls of their stalls and cages. Japheth heard the *thud, thud, thud* as the larger animals hit the walls.

"Father!" Japheth called again. Once again he tried to stand up. With both hands, he grasped the railing that ran along the wall. "Father!" One slow step at a time, Japheth pulled himself along the

THE ARK ROCKED VIOLENTLY.

aisle. He had left his father at the other end of the deck, cleaning out the zebra stalls.

The roar grew louder. Japheth could hardly hear his own thoughts. The ark tipped dangerously. Suddenly Japheth wanted to know where everyone was—Shem and Ham and their wives, as well as his own wife and both his parents. Surely the storm was starting again. What other explanation could there be? Any minute now, he would heard the sound of the water striking the leather roof of the ark, as it had for forty days and forty nights.

In determination, Japheth kept moving. "Father! Father!" The ark rocked from left to right, and Japheth lost his grip on the railing. He tumbled to the floor once more. He got back on his feet as quickly as he could. The howling roar drowned out everything around him.

At last Japheth caught a glimpse of his father moving toward him. They met in the middle of the aisle and embraced.

THE ARK ROCKED FROM LEFT TO RIGHT.

"Father, what is happening?" Japheth asked anxiously. "The rain has been over for months. Why is it storming again?"

Noah shook his head. "There is no storm."

"But the wind, Father!" Japheth said. "What else could it be? The rain this time will be worse than before."

Again Noah shook his head. "There is no storm," he repeated. "There will be no more rain."

"Then tell me what this sound is," Japheth demanded.

"I don't know," Noah admitted. "But it cannot be more rain. God said the rain would stop after forty days and forty nights. And it did stop. God has kept us safe so far, and He will keep us safe until the flood is over."

"We must find out what this wind means," Japheth said. "Come with me to the upper deck. I'll climb the ladder and look out the window."

The wind howled, and the ark pitched from side to side. Slowly, one step at a time, Noah and

"I'LL CLIMB THE LADDER."

Japheth made their way to the upper deck and stumbled to the corner where the ladder hung beneath the window.

Shem was already halfway up the ladder. Ham and the women had gathered as well.

"Come down, Shem," Noah commanded.

"But we must see what is happening," Shem insisted. He climbed a rung higher on the ladder.

"Come down!" Noah repeated. "I will go up and look out the window."

"But, Father," Shem protested, "it will be faster if I—"

Noah waved his hand to say that his son should be silent and obey. Reluctantly, Shem lowered himself rung by rung until he stood on the deck with everyone else.

Noah grasped the sides of the ladder and put his foot on the first rung. He moved steadily but slowly. On the fourth rung, his foot slipped. The whole family gasped. Shem loudly insisted his father should come down, but Noah ignored him.

THE WHOLE FAMILY GASPED.

Noah caught his balance, steadied himself, and began to climb again. He conquered ten rungs, then fifteen, then twenty. Finally he reached the window.

Standing on the top rung of the ladder, Noah pushed his hands on the bottom of the small window and pulled himself up. The opening was barely big enough to put his head through. He knew he would never get his shoulders through. He looked out, past the eaves of the roof, past the edges of the ark, to the water. What he saw made him tighten his grip on the window sill.

"What do you see, Father?" his sons called out. "Tell us what you see."

"God is rolling back the water," Noah answered. "He has sent the wind of His Spirit to push back the water."

"Can you see land?" everyone wanted to know.

"GOD IS ROLLING BACK THE WATER!"

"WE CAN GO BACK TO OUR CHORES."

12

Noah did not see land. But he firmly believed they would see land soon. Just as God had brought the waters, now He would push them away. But there was a lot of water. It might take a very long time.

On the deck below him, his family clung to the walls and railings to keep their balance. Carefully, slowly, Noah lowered himself down the ladder and joined them.

"We can go back to our chores," he told the huddled group. He had to shout to be heard above the wind.

"Just go back to work?" Ham asked, also

shouting. "Like nothing is happening?"

"The animals must be fed. Their stalls must be cleaned," Noah insisted. "I should be finished with the zebras soon."

Japheth began to nod his head slowly. "What you mean, Father, is that you do not know how long this will last. We must carry on with our responsibilities while we wait."

Noah nodded. "That is what I mean. It could be weeks before the water is gone. Go finish feeding the birds. Shem, the big animals may need some new drinking water. I would imagine a lot of the troughs have spilled." Noah ignored his family's stares as he moved past them and began to make his way back to the zebras. He did not look back or say anything more. Slowly, the others followed him back to work.

For days, weeks, months, the family carried on this way. They could hear the wind and knew that the waters were drying up. The ark rocked from side to side. They felt the motion of the

HE BEGAN TO MAKE HIS WAY TO THE ZEBRAS.

swirling water. But how long would it be before they found land?

Then, one day, the ark stopped. The wind stopped. The waters stopped rolling. The ark no longer pitched from side to side. When the hippos and the rhinos and the elephants all moved to one side of the ark, the vessel still stayed flat. Even the woodpecker seemed to sense a change and stopped pecking wood.

Once again, Noah's three sons scrambled to the ladder to see what was happening. And once again, he called them down and insisted on climbing the rungs himself. The anxious family stood below him, waiting for his announcement.

"We are indeed stopped," he shouted, as he looked out the window. "We seem to be on top of a mountain."

"Is there dry land?" Shem asked. "Can you see any land at all?"

Noah scanned the horizon. His view from the small window was limited. But everywhere he

"WE ARE INDEED STOPPED."

looked he saw water. No treetops, no fields, just water. It was as if they were an island in the middle of a vast, unending lake. The blue of the water met the blue of the sky so perfectly that Noah could hardly tell where the water ended and the sky began. As beautiful as it was, he had hoped for something else.

He turned to his family and shook his head. No land, except the very tip of the mountain on which they sat.

So they waited some more. They had already been in the ark for half a year. Japheth had filled a large patch of wall with his scratchings to count the days. Shem and Ham would often go down and recount the marks, as if they could speed the time by finding some mistake in Japheth's arithmetic.

Some of the family were getting restless. They gazed up at the windows, longing to run free and feel the rush of fresh air on their faces. But, as Noah liked to remind his family, where else did they have to go? So they waited. Every day, someone climbed

THE ARK WAS ON THE VERY TOP OF A MOUNTAIN.

the ladder and studied the view. They looked for any spot of brown, a tree trunk, perhaps, or the dirt on the side of the mountain. They looked for anything green, perhaps the budding leaf on a branch or the lush, thick grass of a meadow. For three months they watched and waited.

Finally, the day came that Noah announced he could see the tops of several other mountains below them. Wherever they were, they were very high.

"We're sitting on top of the world," Shem marveled as he looked out one day. He could see nothing around them that was higher than they were.

After they saw the tops of the mountains, Noah began to count the days again. He waited forty days. And then one morning, he said, "Shem, bring me a raven."

With the bird on his shoulder and his family standing on the upper deck, Noah climbed the ladder. At the top, he grasped the bird with both

NOAH CLIMBED THE LADDER!

hands, whispered a prayer for its safety, and tossed it out the window. The black wings opened immediately and began to flap. Noah smiled as the shiny black bird soared against the blue sky. God made birds for flying, he told himself, not for being cooped up within the walls of an ark.

The raven flew back and forth, back and forth. Noah watched it pass the window each time. He turned to his family and shook his head. The raven could find nowhere to land. There was no dry land yet.

They waited again. They fed the animals, cleaned the stalls and tried not to think about how the raven had circled the ark with nowhere else to go.

Then Noah climbed the ladder once more, this time with a dove in his hands. Perhaps by now there would be a treetop where a bird might find a home. He tossed it out the window. Its wings fluttered open, and the dove began to circle. Its shimmering white color was almost lost in the

NOAH HAD A DOVE IN HIS HANDS.

bright sunlight, but Noah kept his eyes fixed on it. It flew east and west; it flew north and south. It circled widely around the ark. But in the end, it came back to Noah at the window. Noah reached out his arm, and the dove gently landed on his hand. The old man pulled it to safety within the upper deck of the ark.

Noah stood at the top of the ladder, with his family waiting below, and stroked the soft feathers of the dove. "Perhaps a few more days," he said softly. "We'll try again in a few more days. You will be the one to tell us about our new home."

He could see the disappointment in the faces of his family. But they had no choice. They would have to wait some more.

"PERHAPS A FEW MORE DAYS."

THE BIRD FLUTTERED ITS WINGS.

13

Seven days later, Noah climbed the ladder with the dove once again. The instant he opened his hand, the bird fluttered its wings and lifted off into the free air. Noah hunched through the window as far as he could to watch where the bird went. Would it circle and come back? Or would it find its freedom in a new life?

The bird was soon out of sight. Noah's heart beat a little faster. The bird did not come back right away as it had the week before, or as the raven had the week before that.

Looking around from the mountain-top perch,

NOAH

Noah could see that the water around them had gone down. Patches of land had appeared on the mountainsides. It was difficult to see anything from the tiny window tucked under the eaves of the ark's roof, but what Noah saw made him hopeful. But they were so high up. They would have to find land at a lower elevation, or there would be no hope of growing food. The family had lived inside the ark among the animals for eleven months. Even Noah, who was more patient than all the others, was ready to get out. He longed to walk on solid ground, to eat fresh vegetables, to pray with his face lifted to the sun.

Noah looked for the dove again. It was nowhere in sight.

"Father, aren't you coming down?" Shem asked.

Noah shook his head. "I'm going to wait for the dove."

"Hasn't it come back?" Shem asked, with a hint of excitement in his voice.

"I'M GOING TO WAIT FOR THE DOVE!"

"No, but it may still come back."

"You'll get tired sitting up on top of the ladder."

"I'll be fine, Shem."

"Mother will not approve."

"No, she won't."

Noah just could not bring himself to leave his watching place. Every minute that the dove stayed out of sight gave him more hope.

The day passed slowly, but at last evening came. Noah's eyes darted around the horizon, looking for the dove. Had it found a treetop where it could build a nest? Had it found enough leaves and branches to use for a nest?

And then the bird came back. It landed softly on Noah's arm. For a moment, Noah's heart sank. He had truly hoped that the bird would not come back this time. And then, Noah looked more closely. The dove's beak was clamped shut around something green.

Noah reached for the bird and pried open its beak.

THE BIRD CAME BACK.

"It's a leaf!" he called down to his family. He started to climb down the ladder. "It's an olive leaf!"

"An olive leaf?" Japheth echoed. "But olive trees do not grow on the tops of mountains. They grow much lower down."

Noah nodded excitedly. "That's right. This little dove has been all the way down the side of the mountain, and he's come back to tell us that the waters are nearly gone."

"Can we leave the ark, then?" Ham asked.

Noah shook his head. "Not yet. We'll wait a few more days. Then we'll send the dove out again. If he doesn't come back, then we'll know the time is right."

So they waited some more. Seven days crawled by. Japheth marked off seven more scratches on his wall. Shem and Ham nervously tried to concentrate on their chores.

Finally Noah climbed the ladder again with the dove and shooed it out the window. Then he

"IT'S AN OLIVE LEAF."

settled on the top of the ladder to wait. The family gathered below. They waited all day and long into the evening. The bird did not come back. The family hardly slept that night. They knew what the dove's absence meant. They knew what the morning would bring. Everyone was up before dawn.

Shem scrambled up the ladder and looked around for the dove. Grinning, he looked down at his anxious family and shook his head. The dove had not returned!

"Throw off the roof," Noah commanded.

His sons needed no further prompting. They shinnied up the walls and tugged at the hides sewn together for the roof. Their muscles rippled as they pulled the hides apart at the seams. Eagerly and joyfully, they rolled the roof back. Sunlight bathed the upper deck of the ark. People and animals alike squinted at the brightness.

"It looks dry, Father!" Japheth called out. He stood at the railing of the ark, looking over the

THEY PULLED THE HIDES APART.

side and studying the ground forty-five feet below him.

Noah nodded, his own excitement shining in his eyes.

"Let's go!" Shem cried. "Come on, Ham, let's open the door on the lower deck." Ham quickly fell into step with Shem, and they ran across the deck to the stairs.

"Wait!" Noah called after his sons. "Not yet."

They stopped and turned to look at him. "The ground is dry, Father. You can see that for yourself."

"I know," Noah answered, "and I want to get off the ark as much as you do. But God has not yet said it is time."

"What do you mean? Are we going to stay here? Keep waiting?"

Noah nodded at his doubtful sons. "That is what we will do."

"But the animals, Father," Shem protested. "It's time for them to move about freely."

"WAIT! NOT YET."

"And for us to do the same!" Japheth added.

"We will wait," Noah said simply.

So they waited. Weeks went by. Japheth scratched off the days. Soon they reached the one-year mark—one year of living inside the ark with the animals.

Noah woke early one morning. As soon as his eyes popped open, he knew he must go down to the lower deck and check the door. As he moved through the aisles on the lower deck, he felt the rush of fresh air. Just as he suspected, the door was open.

"Come out of the ark," a voice said. "You and your wife and your sons and their wives. Bring out every kind of living creature that is with you—the birds, the animals, and all the creatures that move along the ground—so that they can multiply on the earth and be fruitful and increase in number upon it."

Noah strode through the aisles of the decks and threw open the latches on the stalls and

"BRING OUT EVERY KIND OF LIVING CREATURE."

catches. He pulled the doors and gates open. He thumped the rumps of the bigger animals to get them moving. By the time he got to the small monkeys, Shem had discovered what he was doing. Within a few minutes, the whole family was there, shooing animals out of the ark and into the daylight—and onto solid ground.

Some animals went eagerly. Some were not so sure. But with prodding from Noah and his family, they spilled out of the ark and onto the land. The woodpecker whizzed by Japheth's head and disappeared into a thicket of trees.

Japheth roared with laughter. Shem shrieked with delight. Ham whooped with joy. Noah raised his face and smiled at heaven.

THE ANIMALS BEGAN TO LEAVE THE ARK.

HAM CLIMBED THE HIGHEST TREE.

14

Shem rolled in the grass until he was covered in dirt and dew. Ham climbed the tallest tree he could find. Japheth decided that he enjoyed the sound of the woodpecker—in the forest. The women rushed to pick wildflowers blooming on the mountainside and search for the fresh herbs that had been missing from their food for the last year.

The animals kept coming from the ark. They poured out onto the side of the mountain, squinted in the sunlight, and began their new lives. The birds soared in the sky, swirling and swooping before disappearing from sight. The panthers and cheetahs and other animals that were made for fleet running were gone in an instant. Once the grand exit began, no human or animal wanted it to end.

Noah watched it all. Like the rest of his family, he was eager to stand on firm ground again. But he was too old to roll in the grass or climb a tree. He stood outside the ark and watched the excitement around him.

"Where will all the animals go?" Shem asked. "So many of them appeared out of nowhere last year. What if they can't survive around here?"

Noah smiled knowingly. "God will take them back to where they belong."

"So we won't see them again?"

"Perhaps not."

Shem scowled. "I got used to having them around. I'll miss them."

"So will I," said Japheth, as he came up behind them.

THE CHEETAHS WERE GONE IN AN INSTANT.

"Even the woodpecker?" Noah asked, laughing.

"Oh, maybe even the woodpecker!"

Noah raised his hands above his head. "We must thank God for keeping us safe, as well as all the animals—even the woodpecker. Japheth, bring me some stones and some wood. Shem, I'll need some birds for a sacrifice."

"Now I understand why we needed seven of some of the birds," Shem said. "It's so that there will be some to sacrifice and others to breed and multiply."

"That's exactly right," Noah answered. "Let's get busy with this altar."

Soon the whole family was helping to build the altar. The stones were in place, and the fire lit. Noah prepared the birds.

"This is an offering of thanksgiving and dedication," Noah explained. "We will express our gratitude for God's safekeeping for the last year. Then we will dedicate ourselves to serve Him for the rest of our lives."

THE WHOLE FAMILY HELPED BUILD THE ALTAR.

NOAH

The family watched solemnly as Noah sacrificed the birds.

"Listen," Noah said to his family, "and you will hear God speak."

The wind swirled around them, and the smoke from the sacrifice floated upward. And they did hear God speak. The only eight people on earth stood and listened as the God Who cared for them spoke. No one moved a muscle.

"That was a holy moment," Noah said, when it was over. "You must never forget it."

"How could we forget it?" Japheth asked. "We have survived the flood that destroyed the whole earth, and now God has promised that He will never again destroy all living creatures because people are sinful."

"We are still sinful," Noah warned his family. "Just because we have been spared from the flood, we must not think that we are perfect. We are all capable of the cruel and thoughtless things that we saw others do. God has promised not to destroy

THEY STOOD AND LISTENED.

the earth again because of our sin. But we must never forget that we are sinners."

Noah turned away from the altar and opened his arms wide. "We have a whole new world," he said. "God has made a covenant with me, a promise. And He makes it with you, because you are my descendants. And you will have descendants of your own. You must never forget. And you can be sure that God will never forget what He has promised."

"Look!" Shem cried. "In the sky, over there!"

Seven pairs of eyes turned to see what Shem had seen. A band of light, shining with every color they could imagine, bent over the horizon. It sparkled in the sunlight and reflected majestically in the pools and ponds that dotted the mountainside. It disappeared over the horizon and then circled back and surrounded them.

"It's beautiful!" Noah's wife exclaimed.

"It's a rainbow," Noah explained. "The rainbow is God's sign that He will keep His promise.

"IT'S A RAINBOW."

Whenever it appears in the sky, God will remember His promise.

"And so will we," Shem said.

"Yes," Noah agreed. "And so will we."

"GOD WILL REMEMBER HIS PROMISE."

AWESOME BOOKS FOR KIDS!

The Young Reader's Christian Library
Action, Adventure, and Fun Reading!

This series for young readers ages 8 to 12 is action-packed, fast-paced, and Christ-centered! With exciting illustrations on every other page following the text, kids won't be able to put these books down! Over 100 illustrations per book. All books are paperbound. The unique size (4 ⅛" x 5 ⅜") makes these books easy to take anywhere!

A Great Selection to Satisfy All Kids!

Available wherever books are sold.

Or order from: Barbour Publishing, Inc., P.O. Box 719
Uhrichsville, Ohio 44683
http://www.barbourbooks.com

$2.50 each retail, plus $1.00 for postage and handling per order. Prices subject to change without notice.